Deeper Encoun

TOTAL FORGIVENESS

John Wilks

7 studies for leaders of confident small groups
with CD audio tracks and photocopiable worksheets

DEEPER ENCOUNTER: TOTAL FORGIVENESS by John Wilks

Scripture Union, 207–209 Queensway, Bletchley, MK2 2EB, UK
email: info@scriptureunion.org.uk
www.scriptureunion.org.uk

Scripture Union Australia: Locked Bag 2, Central Coast Business Centre, NSW 2252
www.su.org.au

Scripture Union USA: PO Box 987 #1, Valley Forge, PA 19482, USA
www.scriptureunion.org

ISBN 1 84427 236 2
ISBN 978 1 84427 236 5

First published in Great Britain by Scripture Union 2007

© John Wilks

All rights reserved. No part of this publication may be reproduced, stored in a retrieval system, or transmitted, in any form or by any means, electronic, mechanical, photocopying, recording or otherwise, without the prior permission of Scripture Union – the exception being the **photocopiable worksheets** which can be freely photocopied by the leader who has purchased the book.

The right of John Wilks to be identified as author of this work has been asserted by him in accordance with the Copyright, Designs and Patents Act 1988.

Scripture quotations, unless otherwise indicated, are taken from the Holy Bible, New International Version. Copyright © 1973, 1978, 1984 by International Bible Society. Anglicisation copyright © 1979, 1984, 1989. Used by permission of Hodder and Stoughton Limited. Or from the Holy Bible, Today's New International Version, TNIV. Copyright © 2001, 2005 by International Bible Society.

British Library Cataloguing-in-Publication data: a catalogue record for this book is available from the British Library.

Cover design by mhm grax of London

Internal page design by Creative Pages: www.creativepages.co.uk

Printed and bound by goodmanbaylis, The Trinity Press, Worcester and London

Scripture Union is an international Christian charity working with churches in more than 130 countries providing resources to bring the good news about Jesus Christ to children, young people and families – and to encourage them to develop spiritually through the Bible and prayer. As well as co-ordinating a network of volunteers, staff and associates who run holidays, church-based events and school Christian groups, Scripture Union produces a wide range of publications and supports those who use their resources through training programmes.

FOREWORD

'... a unique, insightful and imaginative resource which will help satisfy a growing hunger among mature Christian people ... a series that will nourish serious disciples in our churches.'

If we want to be people who live out our Christian faith with integrity in a complex world, we need to be people who are serious in our engagement with God's Word – following the example of the early Church seekers and disciples who 'every day ... studied the Scriptures' and were 'devoted to the apostles' teaching'.

The great thing about the *Deeper Encounter* series is that it is a stimulating resource honed to fulfil these aims. Challenging central themes about the nature of God and the way of salvation have been selected. We are encouraged to relate the focal passages to both their scriptural and historical contexts. Our individual Christian journeys are properly affirmed and we are encouraged to integrate these with Scripture – yet Scripture is not sacrificed on the altar of the personal or the contemporary. The mix of printed text, audio input via CD and worksheets means that interest is sustained and stimulated.

This is a series that will nourish serious disciples in our churches, enabling us to respond by informing our minds with God's truth, opening our hearts to God's light, shaping our wills by God's ways, and above all learning to relate more deeply to who God is – his character as revealed in Scripture.

The Rev Dr David Spriggs
Head of Church Relations, Bible Society

Welcome!

This series of small group studies is particularly aimed at confident small groups: groups of about 6 to 12 people who have a good general grounding in Bible knowledge and who are ready for a more demanding study with searching questions. In fact, the quality of the interactive question times is one of the strong distinctives of the *Deeper Encounter* series. This feature will appeal to groups who have grown tired of more predictable question-and-answer sessions and need to move on to the kind of discussion that leaves everyone stimulated and energised.

Each of these seven studies follows a flexible pattern that will be described in the Introduction that follows. Integral and vital to the studies is the extra material on the CD. Three clips are to be played at the appointed times during each session. They provide valuable width to the study, and I trust will also give real enjoyment.

Although not spoken by the author but by a professional actor, the CD tracks will enable the groups to experience a level of relationship with John Wilks through his words which I know will be one of the rewarding aspects of the material. John is Director of Open Learning at the London School of Theology (formerly London Bible College) and his experience makes him the ideal writer of material for a group that wants to go deeper into the biblical material and with a strong focus on application. He has an impressive ability to be very challenging in the area of application – beyond the obvious! And he brings a creativity and liveliness to the study not always found in theological material! John is married to Joanne and together they have seven children, ranging from early twenties to five years old. He is the pianist and one of the preachers at a community church they helped to establish in 1991. I know you will enjoy getting to know him through these studies.

If you benefit from this study I hope you will move on to others in the series. Details of other titles are given at the back of the book.

You will have noticed that the series is branded with the logo of *Encounter with God*, a quarterly personal Bible reading guide publication from Scripture Union which it is my privilege to edit. *Deeper Encounter* is aimed at the same kind of readership as *Encounter with God*, so if you have gained from using this material in a small group you are warmly invited to look at using the Bible reading guide to which it is a companion if you don't do so already. Again, you'll find full details at the back of this book.

Finally, it is often said that small group leaders are some of the unsung heroes of church life. The small group is where many people spend their most significant times around God's Word. We hope that *Deeper Encounter* will help you in your important task of communicating to them the truth and relevance of the Bible. May God's Spirit equip and enable you as you lead them through *Total Forgiveness*.

Andrew Clark
Editor, *Encounter with God*

Introduction: Total Forgiveness

A major aim of this *Deeper Encounter* study booklet is that our spirituality and our personal relationship with God should deepen and grow. It will focus on our confidence in God's forgiveness of our sins. At its core, there are two aspects of our forgiveness: that we simply need to confess sin, and that we must forgive others who sin against us. The reality of this is sometimes much more challenging, both in facing up to our own persistent sinfulness and the magnitude of sin and its abhorrent nature. We will consider the place of repentance, of restoration and of making recompense within the uncomplicated basic statement of 1 John 1:9: 'If we confess our sins, he is faithful and just and will forgive us our sins and purify us from all unrighteousness.'

Each of these seven studies follows a flexible pattern. There is a **Leader's briefing** which is designed to equip group leaders to approach the session and should not be read to the group; and there are interactive question sections under the headings of **Investigation** and **Application**. The questions which prompt these discussion times are repeated (without leader's notes) on the **Photocopiable worksheets** at the back of the book. As leader you can decide whether to give out these worksheets in advance or at the beginning of each session. Some groups will be very ready to do a little 'homework' in preparation for the session; others may find this commitment too much of a burden.

In addition, there are audio tracks from the CD for each session. The **Preparation** track is mainly scene-setting; the **Observation** track will give extra insights and reflections from my own experience; and the **Summary** will highlight the major points of the session.

Whenever I make reference to something in one of the audio tracks – be it to a Bible verse, song, hymn, film, event or individual – you will find the reference included in the book. Then, if anyone wants to ask questions about it, you will have the information you need.

Each session concludes with a brief and optional **Reflection and adoration** section. Your knowledge of the group will help you to decide which, if any, of the suggested elements of prayer and worship would be appropriate to use or adapt to close the session.

Finally, each session includes an optional **Continuation** section. This gives ideas of things that the group members can do in the days that follow the session in order to reinforce the study material. Rather than involving further Bible study, these suggestions use resources such as films and books that explore similar themes to those that have been discussed. They are intended to be simultaneously relaxing and thought-provoking.

Contacting me

If you wish, you can contact me in one of two ways. You can visit my blog on

http://homepage.mac.com/wilksenterprise/blogwavestudio/index.html

or send an email to

wilksenterprise@mac.com

On the blog you will hear me describing the process of writing further books, and have the opportunity to comment on that process. In addition, you will be able to let me know how your sessions went, and pass on any encouragements or frustrations you have found. Finally, there is information not only about *Deeper Encounter* but also about other aspects of my work and interests. I cannot guarantee to respond to every email or comment personally, but certainly look forward to your input.

John Wilks

Contents

Welcome!		4
Introduction: Total Forgiveness		5
1	Confess and be forgiven	9
2	Total confession	14
3	Continual forgiveness	18
4	Making recompense	22
5	Forgiven much, love much	26
6	Neither do I condemn you	31
7	The joy of your salvation	35
Photocopiable worksheets		39

Please note: All worksheet pages at the back of this book are photocopiable; alternatively, they are accessible as PDF files from the audio CD for you to print out locally.

1: CONFESS AND BE FORGIVEN

1 JOHN 1:5 – 2:2

Leader's briefing

The starting point for this series on the subject of forgiveness is the simplicity of what we need to do in order to be forgiven. Contrary to the idea that there might be a number of different things someone might need to do in order to merit forgiveness, the Bible is clear that not only is there nothing we can do to merit forgiveness but actually very little is required of us. Because Christ's death on the cross has done so much of what is necessary, all we need do is acknowledge that we have sinned, and ask to be forgiven – so little and yet, for many, too much.

This is one of those aspects of the Christian life that can take years or even decades to sink into a Christian's mentality. Even if we know it intellectually, ironically we can still hold the unexpressed opinion that because forgiveness is not deserved, therefore it is unobtainable.

Now, we all know that there are additional nuances to add to the topic of forgiveness that make things not quite so straightforward. I would therefore encourage you to assure group members that these will be discussed in later sessions. For the moment, it is important that the lack of complication in the words of John's First Letter is heard and accepted at face value. God does not want us to sacrifice our children in order to gain forgiveness (see Micah 6:7).

The **Observation** track introduces the idea that sin is one of the least important things in the Christian life. This self-evidently radical expression is designed to bring out the totality of Christ's work for us. It is not intended to belittle the seriousness of sin, but to express the seriousness of Christ's work. If forgiveness really is that readily available, then perhaps God wants us to accept it readily and move on to enjoy our relationship with him. Don't be worried if you need to play the **Observation** track again if group members are a little thrown by the idea at first.

Preparation

Play CD track 1.

Read 1 John 1:1 – 2:2. Make it clear to the group members that the first four verses are not part of the study and are being read only to establish the context.

Investigation

1. What does John mean by the phrase 'walk in the darkness'? If we commit a single sin does that mean that we are then walking 'in the darkness'? Or does he have something different in mind?

2. Think about the people who claimed to be 'without sin' (verses 8 and 10). What might they have understood about the Christian life to have so deluded themselves into genuinely believing this was correct? Alternatively, do we think they were maliciously trying to deceive people?

3. Most of the New Testament letters were written to challenge incorrect ideas that had developed. Looking at the things John writes here, what wrong ideas do we think his audience had started believing?

Note: The most obvious error is that Christians are free from sin, in the sense that a Christian cannot commit sin. Perhaps this arose from misunderstanding baptism as an act that somehow makes us incapable of sin rather than saying it cleanses us from sin. A different nuance of the same idea could be a belief that the Christian does not actually have to confess their sin because Jesus' death has already paid the price for it. In other words, since the penalty is already paid, even when a Christian sins the mark of that sin only remains on them for a moment before God has forgiven it (without the need for them to request forgiveness).

Optional extra question:

4. In Micah 6:7 we read, 'Shall I offer my firstborn for my transgression, the fruit of my body for the sin of my soul?' What misconceptions about forgiveness and God's requirements of us are common in today's Church?

Observation

Play CD track 2. Give the group a chance to ask any questions to clarify what they have just heard.

Application

5. Is it possible to make too much of sin and confession in the

Christian life? What might be the dangers of this?

6   Does our local church make too much, or too little, of sin and confession in our services?

7   Does the idea that sin is the *least* important thing in the Christian life mean that we can commit any sins we want?

8   What things, if any, worry us about the idea that sin might be the least important thing in the Christian life? What issues and/or balancing statements would we want to see in later sessions?

Note: It would be a good idea to jot these questions down in the book. Do point out to group members that we're not going to try to answer these issues now, since we hope that they will be covered in the coming sessions.

9   How would we know if we ought to be paying more (or less) attention to the sin in our lives?

Note: Differences here are probably more to do with our differing personality types. I would suggest that we need to ask whether we pay too little attention to sin because we are blasé about God forgiving us whatever we do, and whether we pay too much attention because we are not confident and certain of the straightforward statement of 1 John 1:9.

10   What sort of things might make us unwilling to admit even to ourselves that we have sinned?

11   What is the proper role of guilt in the Christian life?

12   Do you think that in his letter John is trying to make us feel guilty about sin?

13   How have we dealt with any guilt we feel even after we have confessed our sins? Without needing to go into details of the sin, would anyone be willing to share what they did to alleviate any lingering sense of guilt?

Summary

Play CD track 3.

Texts mentioned:

–   'Had I, myself, really ever dared to step into the center, kneel down, and let myself be held by a forgiving God?' – Henri Nouwen, *The Return of the Prodigal Son*, Darton, Longman & Todd, 1992, p12.

- 'What shall we say, then? Shall we go on sinning, so that grace may increase?' – Romans 6:1.
- 'But seek first his kingdom and his righteousness… ' – Matthew 6:33.

Reflection and adoration

As an optional way of closing each session of this study series, there will be an opportunity to focus on one area of our relationships with other people. I encourage you to allow time for personal reflection and prayer, focusing on the particular category of people suggested. For this first session, the group members might think about relationships in their church. Are there relationships that need a word of forgiveness? Relationships that we can be joyful about after their restoration as a result of confession and forgiveness?

Please assure group members that this is not about attempting to exert pressure or guilt, but to give an opportunity for prayerful reflection. We should think over the times when we have experienced forgiveness for sins we have committed or extended forgiveness to those who sinned against us, and ask God to bring to mind any situation where we need to forgive other people. That may necessitate us speaking to the other person, or it may not; let us ask God for guidance on how to act.

You may like to close with a meditative reading of this verse from the Charles Wesley hymn 'Jesus, lover of my soul', which emphasises our dependence on God for everything:

> Other refuge have I none,
>> hangs my helpless soul on Thee;
> Leave, ah! leave me not alone,
>> still support and comfort me.
> All my trust on Thee is stayed,
>> all my help from Thee I bring;
> Cover my defenceless head
>> with the shadow of Thy wing.

Continuation

If you would like to take the subject of this series further, then a spiritually profound book that will richly repay the time spent on it is Henri Nouwen's *The Return of the Prodigal Son* (Darton, Longman & Todd, 1992). It combines a meditation on the familiar parable with reflections on the Rembrandt oil painting of the same name. The book is very easy to read, being full of anecdotes and personal reflections alongside rich theological insights.

With the same title as this study series, RT Kendall's *Total Forgiveness* (Hodder & Stoughton, 2001) is another to consider. A more challenging but very rewarding academic book would be Miroslav Volf's *Exclusion and Embrace* (Abingdon, 1996). A theologian from Croatia, Volf needed to come to terms with the treatment of Croatians by Serbians during the 1990s. He found the solution in the willingness of God to embrace an enemy, so giving us an image of how to treat those who oppose us.

There are many books that could be recommended; in fact, I lost track of the number of people who recommended (or insisted) that I read a particular book whenever I mentioned that I was writing a book on forgiveness! So if I've not listed your favourite it's not because I disapprove of it, it's simply that space is limited. Perhaps group members could all bring their favourite book on the topic and swap with one another?

For a film on the theme of forgiveness, an obvious starting point would be *End of the Spear* (2006, directed by Jim Hanon). The story of Jim Elliot and four other missionaries who were attacked and murdered by the Auca tribesmen of Ecuador they had intended to evangelise is well known from the books written by his wife Elisabeth. The film continues the story into the reconciliation and forgiveness that developed between Steve Saint, the son of the pilot who took the missionaries into the jungle (and was killed along with them), and Mincayini, one of the murderers.

2: TOTAL CONFESSION

PSALM 32:1–5

Leader's briefing

After the basic statement of the simplicity of forgiveness, we turn now to a group of three studies that look at some of the problems. They do not change the truth of 1 John; rather, they act as checks on a flippant attitude that might develop. So we will be thinking about emotions, the importance of repentance and forgiving others, and about making recompense.

Mature Christians should be well aware (intellectually) that while expressing our emotions is not necessarily a bad thing, there is the potential for it to be harmful or beneficial. There are probably times when our emotions get the better of us; we can be all too aware of what we ought to do, but reluctant to do it. Psalm 32 seems to be describing such an experience, with a good deal of detail about the psychosomatic effects this turmoil can have on us.

Into this mix we need to add repentance – turning away from sin and towards God. Given its association with a conversion experience, some people may feel that repentance has no ongoing role in the Christian life. Others, by contrast, may feel that it has a role, but one that is driven by emotional response. A third view is that repentance is something Christians should do frequently (and with no implications of a merely emotional reaction), if not every time they confess their sins to God. This session will help us think through those ideas.

Preparation

Play CD track 4.

Read the whole of Psalm 32, even though we will only be studying the first five verses.

Investigation

1. Why might we be unwilling to acknowledge our sin to God? Psychologically speaking, what might be happening to make us reluctant to own up to sin?

2. Does the phrase 'in whose spirit there is no deceit' (verse 2) describe some sort of excellent sinlessness, or does it refer to something else?

3. Have any of us experienced this 'groaning' and 'wasting away' (verse 3)?

4. Is the psalmist describing psychosomatic illness or just using poetic language? Does it matter which it is?

5. What do we think the 'guilt of my sin' (verse 5) is?

6. The **Preparation** audio track also mentioned times when we do not feel any sort of negative emotion about our sins. Can we still be forgiven for them, and – if so – on what basis?

7. Verses 1 and 2 describe a blessed state for those who have sinned and confessed; is this a good motivation for us to confess our sins to God, that we might feel good as a result?

Read Matthew 5:23,24.

8. What contemporary situations would parallel the inconvenience of leaving a sacrifice in order to be reconciled with someone? How far does Jesus expect us to go?

Observation

Play CD track 5. Give the group a chance to ask any questions to clarify what they have just heard.

Texts mentioned:

– 'Confession is like opening the floodgate of a dam. When there is no confession, the waters pile up behind the dam, creating immense pressures on the wall, but as soon as the floodgate is opened, the waters subside and the pressures diminish' – Peter Craigie, *Psalms 1–50, Word Biblical Commentary*, Word, 1983, p267.

– 'But when you are tempted, he will also provide a way out so that you can stand up under it' – 1 Corinthians 10:13.

Application

9. Do we recognise ourselves in these attempts to justify not confessing our sins?

– 'Look, Lord, I've committed this one so often I don't really need to confess it again.'

- 'I might as well wait until I've committed this one a few more times and then confess them all as a sort of job lot.'

What other reasons do any of us have for not being willing to confess our sins?

10   How would we define repentance?
- Is repentance something we do once, when we become Christians, or something that should be a frequent part of the Christian life? Or are they two different things that we could do with different terms for?
- Is repentance something that comes out of an emotional response to sin, or is it more an intellectual decision?
- Is repentance the same as remorse and penitence for our sins?
- What is the difference between asking for forgiveness and repenting?

Note: Theologian Wayne Grudem defines repentance as, 'a heartfelt sorrow for sin, a renouncing of it, and a sincere commitment to forsake it and walk in obedience to Christ' (*Systematic Theology*, IVP, 1994, p713). It is a topic that is very important at the start of our Christian life, but group members may have different opinions on its continuing role in the ongoing Christian life. Rather than limit discussion by telling you what I think, I encourage the group to discuss the reasons for their different opinions, and to seek common ground between them.

11   What experience of trusting in the promise in 1 Corinthians 10:13 have we had which we can share with one another?

Note: Lest the connection between repentance and 1 Corinthians 10:13 seems a little obscure, the connection I see is all about not continuing to sin. Repentance is setting ourselves to avoid sin; trusting in the Holy Spirit for the way of escape when faced with the sin is how we can fulfil our determination to live a holy life.

Summary

Play CD track 6.

Texts mentioned:

- 'Sin, the world and the devil' – from the Anglican rite of Baptism – 'and do sign him with the sign of the Cross, in token that hereafter he shall not be ashamed to confess the faith of Christ crucified, and manfully to fight under his banner, against sin, the world, and the

devil; and to continue Christ's faithful soldier and servant until his life's end.'
- 'Because I do not hope to turn again… ' – the opening line of TS Eliot's poem 'Ash Wednesday'.

Reflection and adoration

The second group of people for group members to think about are friends and neighbours outside the Church. Again, this is not meant to be about pressure or guilt, but an opportunity for prayerful reflection. We should think over the times when we have experienced forgiveness for sins we have committed and extended forgiveness for those who sinned against us, and ask God to bring to mind any situation for which we need to forgive other people. Then, praise God for all that he has done in Christ to bless us with cleansing and forgiveness.

Close by singing a hymn or song about repentance and forgiveness. Suggestions include: the Charles Wesley hymn 'And can it be'; 'Dear Lord and Father of mankind' by John Greenleaf Whittier; 'God forgave my sin (Freely, freely)' by Carol Owens © 1972 Bud John Songs/ Universal Songs; 'God of grace (I stand complete in you)' by Chris Bowater © Sovereign Lifestyle Music Ltd; or 'Only by grace' by Gerrit Gustafson © 1990 Integrity's Hosanna Music.

Continuation

Worth watching is the film *Forgiveness* (South Africa, 2004, directed by Ian Gabriel). A policeman revisits the township where he brutally murdered a young activist during the Apartheid years, seeking forgiveness.

Alternatively, *The Straight Story* (1999, director David Lynch, U certificate) recounts the true story of a 73-year-old man who rode his lawn tractor on a slow trip across the USA, seeking to be reconciled to his dying 75-year-old brother.

3: CONTINUAL FORGIVENESS

MATTHEW 6:12–15; 18:21–35

Leader's briefing

The second issue we need to deal with is the expectation that we must forgive other people if we ourselves are to be forgiven by God. Jesus' words on the subject are every bit as straightforward as those in John's First Letter. Only those who forgive others can expect to be forgiven themselves.

But this is precisely the sort of statement that is easy to hold people to ransom with. Well-meaning church pastors and counsellors have been known to so emphasise the necessity of forgiveness that it starts to look as if an unwillingness to forgive is a greater sin than that perpetrated on the person! We will deal with that issue in more depth in the next study; for the moment we will concentrate on the ordinary expectations that God has of us.

In the passage for study, Jesus tells a parable in response to a proposal on forgiveness from Peter. The parable raises the issue in terms of frequency; we can extend that to think about types of sins. Are there certain sins that we find especially difficult to forgive? That is probably a personal issue, and things that one group member will find especially challenging will quite probably be things that a different member sees no particular problem with. Please encourage compassion among group members over this. This subject is very likely to stir up old memories for group members, and you need to be prepared to deal with long-harboured resentments and bitterness that might surface – or not! People can be amazingly resilient in holding on to their hurts, so please do not force issues.

Just in case someone wants to know, there were 6000 denarii to the talent, and a denarius was the typical day's wage for a field labourer (DA Hagner, *Matthew 14–28, Word Biblical Commentary*, Word, 1995, p539).

Preparation

Play CD track 7.

Read Matthew 6:9–15 (though we are really only focusing on verses 12–15) and 18:21–35.

Investigation

1 Do these two passages teach that we are forgiven our sins *because* we forgive others?

2 Do they teach that God cannot possibly forgive us *unless* we have forgiven others?

Note: The following comment may be of interest: 'One should, however, not press the tense of 'have forgiven' (6:12), as if God must wait to forgive until human beings have forgiven others. This verse is not a precise statement of theology but moral exhortation, and 18:23–35 teaches that God's mercy is the prior fact' (WD Davies and Dale C Allison, *Matthew: A Shorter Commentary*, T&T Clark, 2004, p95). At the same time, we should not forget that in the parable the unforgiving servant was punished for his unwillingness to forgive. The questions and comment remind us that God is very eager and willing to forgive, and might even do so ahead of our schedule, but expects his people to act in the same way he does: with outrageous generosity.

3 It seems it was easy for the king/master in Matthew 18 to write off a debt of a million pounds. Do we fall into the same trap of forgiving people when it costs us little (relatively speaking), but holding a grudge when it would be costly for us?

4 In the parable, the debt that needed to be forgiven was financial. What sorts of debts/sins do we find it easy or hard to forgive?

5 In the parable, the king does not forgive the servant a second time. Is that in conflict with the idea that we should forgive 'seventy-seven times' (verse 22)?

Read Luke 17:3b,4. If you have time, you could also read the following verses, which all deal with similar issues: Mark 11:25,26, Ephesians 4:32 and Colossians 3:13.

6 We know Jesus is not asking us to keep count. Is there anything we've said so far that these verses would challenge us with?

Observation

Play CD track 8. Give the group a chance to ask any questions to clarify what they have just heard.

Texts mentioned:

- 'For in the same way as you judge others, you will be judged' – Matthew 7:2.

Application

7. So where are our limits on forgiveness, and what might we find it hard to forgive?

8. Is it harder to forgive people who commit sins against our loved ones than to forgive them for sins committed against us personally? Why is that?

9. How do we continue to forgive someone who sins against us so often that we get exasperated with them as they break the 'seventy-seven times' barrier, or sin against us eight times in one day?

10. Does the length of time that's elapsed since a sin was committed make a difference to our ability to forgive?

11. Under what circumstances (if ever) would it be correct to try to force someone to forgive?

12. Thinking back to the previous session, Psalm 32 described the emotional and physical turmoil that might result from not confessing our own sin to God. Is there an equivalent turmoil when we are not prepared to forgive someone?

Summary

Play CD track 9.

Reflection and adoration

The group of people for prayerful consideration in this session are church leaders. When these people make decisions about our church that we do not agree with, they sometimes hurt us in ways that they do not appreciate. But there are also many church members who hurt their leaders by the quick and blunt way they criticise things that happen in the church. Let us prayerfully think over both aspects of our relationship with our church leaders, present and past, as well as thanking God for all of them and their various gifts.

Then, you could say or sing together 'How can I be free from sin? (Lead me to the cross)' by Graham Kendrick © 1991 Make Way Music, concentrating particularly on the second verse which talks of the 'peace within' which results from experiencing the 'all-forgiving love from the Father's heart to me'.

Continuation

Don't forget the books mentioned at the end of the first session. Because they do not relate specifically to the other sessions they have not been listed. However, that does not mean that they were only relevant at the start.

I recommend the film *Flatliners*, 1990, directed by Joel Schummacher, starring Kiefer Sutherland, Julia Roberts and Kevin Bacon; 15 certificate. A group of medical students experiment with near-death experiences, only to find traumatic events from their past (both things done to them and things they have done) start to overwhelm them. Please note that there are two scenes of a sexual nature in the first half-hour.

4: MAKING RECOMPENSE

LUKE 19:1–10

Leader's briefing

The middle session brings us to the third issue that we are exploring as a nuance of the simple statement in John's First Letter that if we confess our sins, we will be forgiven and cleansed. In this session we will be thinking about the role of making recompense, and how forgiveness and restoration differ (if at all).

The motivation for this session comes from the particularly challenging sinful situations that have become more public over recent decades. Incest, for example, is hardly something new, but the fact that it is found among church members and leaders is certainly something we have had to face up to. Then there are husbands – even so-called Christian husbands – who abuse and dominate their wives. Unfortunately, some church people are insistent that these victims should forgive the perpetrators of these crimes: forgive, or your heavenly Father will not forgive you. As I've already mentioned, sometimes it seems that an unwillingness to forgive is seen as a greater crime than the original offence!

In this situation, the example of Zacchaeus, who voluntarily made recompense for his sins, can be a valuable corrective. His sins were far from petty, and would have caused significant misery and suffering; well aware of this, he acts to undo some of the damage he has done. Sometimes we also need to make recompense. This is more than simply doing something to prove that we're sorry and penitent; it might well be something restorative that is significantly costly for us.

Alongside the restoration of the sinner, there is the issue of a restored relationship. When sin has caused some breakdown in relationship, how quickly should we expect to see a return to the original relationship? If we only think about relatively straightforward situations, then we will have one answer to that question. If we are more aware of the extreme situations that some people – perhaps even group members? – have to deal with, we may well have a very different answer. Group members will need to show sensitivity to one another as these matters are discussed.

This session is heavily weighted towards the **Application** section, so don't be too worried if the discussion of the **Investigation** question is over fairly quickly. If anything, make sure that you move on to the later section sooner rather than later.

Preparation

Play CD track 10.

Read Luke 19:1–10

Investigation

To start with, a few quick questions on verse 8. Zacchaeus gave away half his possessions and paid back fourfold the money he had cheated people of.

1. Did Jesus ask him to do this?

Note: The passage does not say, and that is the point. We cannot assert that Jesus must have done so.

2. Was he forgiven *because* he did it? If not, why – then – did he do it?
3. What role does making recompense have to play in Christian forgiveness?

Observation

Play CD track 11. Give the group a chance to ask any questions to clarify what they have just heard.

Texts mentioned:

– 'Love means never having to say you're sorry' – *Love Story*, 1970, directed by Arthur Hiller, based on the novel by Erich Segal. By the way, it's probably a red herring to get into a conversation on the validity of this statement!

Application

4. Zacchaeus voluntarily paid compensation for the sin of cheating people out of money. What kind of sins committed by people today might need to be accompanied by some sort of compensation if forgiveness is to be extended?
5. Is there a difference between forgiveness and restoration, and (if so) how does it help us better understand forgiveness?

6 If someone who has committed a crime that ought to be reported to the police asks for forgiveness, should we still report that crime?

7 Do we have the right to ask for some sort of compensation before we are willing to forgive someone?

8 'I just want to pay the price and move on.' Are there times when we simply cannot deal with our sins and failures just by making recompense?

9 In the previous session we heard the idea that people sometimes say, 'I'll never forgive you for that.' Have any of us ever had that said to us, and, if so, what did we do (if anything) to try to make good the damage and hurt?

10 Will anyone in the group admit to having said, 'I'll never forgive you/him/her for that'? Do they still feel the same way?

Summary

Play CD track 12.

Texts mentioned:

- Scepticism over the reality of Paul's conversion – Acts 9:26,27.

Reflection and adoration

For the prayer time, I suggest that group members focus on their fathers. We hear a great deal about the negative impact that a poor relationship with our father can have. But it is also important for us to acknowledge the benefits of a healthy relationship with our fathers, and thank God for them. In addition, we might want to consider how we might have failed them and need forgiveness from them, as well as ways in which they may need forgiveness from us.

Close by singing about the perfect Fatherhood of God. Some suggested hymns or songs would be 'Dear Lord and Father of mankind' by John Greenleaf Whittier; 'Father God, I wonder (I will sing your praises)' by Ian Smale © 1984 Kingsway's Thankyou Music; 'Father in heaven, how we love you (Blessed be the Lord God Almighty)' by Bob Fitts © 1985 Scripture in Song; 'Father, I place into your hands' by Jenny Hewer © 1975 Kingsway's Thankyou Music.

Continuation

Picking up the theme of fathers from the **Reflection and adoration** section, the suggested film is *Smoke Signals* (1998, director Chris Eyre;

PG certificate), written and directed by a Native American. A young man goes in search of his lost father, who walked out on the family ten years earlier. A reflection on forgiveness within a family, and forgiveness of nations and races. Contains humour, not just earnest and intense scenes.

If this is not available (or to your taste), you might try *The Royal Tenenbaums* (2001, starring Gene Hackman, Angelica Houston, Gwyneth Paltrow and others; 15 certificate). A father estranged from his family fakes a terminal illness, attempting to gain acceptance from them. Predominantly a comedy, it avoids the sentimental and has several dark moments.

5: FORGIVEN MUCH, LOVE MUCH

LUKE 7:36–50

Leader's briefing

I had initially intended that this should be a fairly comforting and encouraging session, not a challenging one. The reality has turned out very differently. These next two sessions form a pair that deal with a different sort of challenge from those we have considered in the previous three. We now turn to consider how we forgive and relate to people who have been found guilty of sins that many of us find difficult to forgive: murder and adultery.

In the **Observation** audio track I will quote the words of two prisoners; one is anonymous, the other – Myra Hindley – is notorious, in Great Britain at least. They describe their own experiences of coming to terms with their crimes, and of the lack of forgiveness for them. They form a curious contrast with the woman described in the Gospels, who so flouts cultural convention in her desire to express her thankfulness for her forgiveness.

Between them, these people enable us to see if we are more like the woman with the perfume or Simon lounging at the meal and making judgements on those around him.

As indicated, the inclusion of these comments from two prisoners means that the session took on a character that I had not initially intended. I have therefore included 'general' **Application** questions as well as some that focus on the implications arising from the prisoners' stories. You may well find that you have a group member who is very resistant to the idea of discussing possible forgiveness for Myra Hindley. Rather than pursue the issue, the general questions should still allow you to continue the session without direct discussion of Hindley.

Preparation

Play CD track 13.

Texts mentioned:

- 'If we confess our sins, he is faithful and just and will forgive us our

sins and purify us from all unrighteousness' – 1 John 1:9.
- 'For if you forgive others when they sin against you, your heavenly Father will also forgive you' – Matthew 6:14.

Read Luke 7:36–50.

Investigation

1. There is a lot of money mentioned in this narrative: a debt of 500 denarii (nearly two years' wages), a debt of 50 denarii (about two months' wages) and an alabaster jar of perfume that in Mark 14:5 is stated as being worth more than a year's wages. What would be an equivalent of a jar of perfume?

2. Do you think the woman has already experienced forgiveness, and wishes to express her gratitude to Jesus, or has she come seeking forgiveness?

3. Is Jesus' parable an absolute statement about forgiveness and love that is applicable in each and every single situation to everyone, or is it one composed for the situation to help Simon see that the woman behaved this way out of gratitude? What difference does it make?

4. Is Jesus telling us to believe that some sins are minor in God's eyes?

5. What ways of misreading the parable can we see?

Note: Among other potential misreadings, here are some from me:

- People who are not overtly demonstrative in their expression of their gratitude to God do not really love him.
- God is not interested in 'minor' sinners, since they don't love him that much.

6. Has our discussion and understanding of forgiveness in any way compromised the straightforward statement of 1 John 1:8,9? If so, what alterations do we need to acknowledge?

Observation

Play CD track 14. Give the group a chance to ask any questions to clarify what they have just heard.

Texts mentioned:

- 'What do you do when you are not forgiven? Society sure [sic] won't forgive us. And I have apologized in writing to the family of my victim a couple of times but with no response. And you know what, I have to admit that if I was in their place, I wouldn't forgive me either. Every year at the anniversary of his death that family grieves it all over again. So I've tried to do the right thing, but how do you stay motivated to seek forgiveness when it never comes?' – F LeRon Shults and Steven J Sandage, *The Faces of Forgiveness: Searching for Wholeness and Salvation*, Baker Book House, 2003, pp64,65.

– 'The truth of this continuing saga/cum Gothic soap opera is that the majority of people don't want to accept that people like myself can change. They prefer to keep me frozen in time together with that awful mugshot so that their attitudes, beliefs and perceptions can remain intact, to preclude the distasteful necessity of considering causes rather than the effects of the roots of the disease, rather than symptoms which are visible' – Myra Hindley, from an article published in *The Guardian*, 18 December 1995, p11.

Application

Questions focusing on forgiveness for crimes:

7 What response would we give to the prisoner who finds his attempts at expressing repentance ignored?

8 In what sense are we required to forgive someone who has not committed their sin against us personally? Would there be mileage in suggesting that some sins are so public that they impact an entire society?

Note: It is very easy for us to see ourselves as so independent that the only things we need to consider are those that impact us directly. If we have a stronger sense of community, then we may be more ready to accept the idea that public crimes are committed against society.

9 When Myra Hindley died, the *Sun* newspaper celebrated the event by declaring its confidence that she was now in hell. Is our ability to forgive someone such as Hindley an appropriate litmus test of our ability to forgive?

10 Which of these other categories of people challenge our ability to forgive them?
  – suicide bombers
  – IRA bombers
  – paedophiles
  – wife batterers

11 What other crimes do we find especially difficult to forgive?

12 There have been a number of public apologies (or not) for acts of violence that took place decades or centuries ago, normally concerning the Holocaust, American slave trade or the Crusades. Does this give us a model for confession of sins we did not commit (but benefit from) and forgiveness of sins committed against others in our society?

13 Presuming that Myra Hindley genuinely repented and asked God to forgive her, is there any reason for believing that she was not forgiven? What are the implications that arise from that?

General questions:

14 Is it essential to have committed (and been forgiven for) 'great' sins in order to 'love much'? Is it enough to be aware of an increasing number of 'minor' sins?

Note: This question raises issues such as the definition of sin, and quite what 'great' and 'minor' sins are anyway. For the moment, I suggest you treat this in a colloquial manner, rather than spending time on a subject that really needs another study series to answer.

15 How do we stop ourselves becoming blasé about our forgiveness?

16 Is it possible to say we have been forgiven if the person we have wronged refuses to forgive us?

17 Have we hurt people in the past by deliberately refusing to forgive them for something?

18 'My chains fell off, my heart was free; I rose, went forth, and followed Thee' (from 'And can it be', Charles Wesley's hymn). Should we think of ourselves as bound in chains whenever we need to be forgiven, or is it only something that was true of our pre-Christian state?

Summary

Play CD track 15.

Texts mentioned:

- 'My own conscience and acute awareness of my own culpability tell me the unpalatable truth that – excepting God's mercy – I have no excuses or explanations to absolve me from my behaviour after the first offence. I knew that what I was involved in was indefensible in every respect; I know the difference between right and wrong and I cared deeply about that difference, though I locked those feelings away. I never attempted to justify my actions either to myself or to Ian Brady, and in all these respects I was the more culpable of the two' – Myra Hindley, from the article already referred to, in *The Guardian*, 18 December 1995, p11.

- '... anyone who looks at a woman lustfully has already committed adultery with her in his heart' – Matthew 5:28.
- 'And anyone who says, "You fool!" will be in danger of the fire of hell' – Matthew 5:22.

Reflection and adoration

I suggest that group members focus on prayer for their mothers. We are sometimes less aware that some people have very much poorer relationships with their mother than with their father. In our meditation, let us keep a balance between how our mothers have failed us, how we have failed them, and how thankful we are for the good things we have received from them.

Close with a song or hymn about the mercy of God, such as: 'Amazing grace' by John Newton; 'God of grace (I stand complete in you)' by Chris Bowater © 1990 Sovereign Lifestyle Music; 'I know not why God's wondrous grace' by DW Whittle, adapted by Stuart Townend © 1999 Thankyou Music; 'I will sing of the mercies' by James H Fillmore; or 'You did not wait for me (I'm for ever grateful)' by Mark Altrogge © 1985 People of Destiny International.

Continuation

After a session that considered prisoners and murder, there are two films worth watching. If you're willing to tackle a foreign-language film you should try *La Veuve de Sainte-Pierre* (*The Widow of Sainte-Pierre*, Canada 2000, director Patrice Leconte, starring Juliet Binochet; 15 certificate). Set in 1849, a man sentenced to death by guillotine (the widow of the film's title) is befriended by the wife of the captain who is guarding him. She rehabilitates him and changes the community's attitude to him.

Alternatively, our suggested film is *The Spitfire Grill* (1996, writer and director Lee David Zlotoff, 12 certificate). The arrival of a young woman who has recently been released from prison stirs up feelings and resentment in the town of Gilead.

6: NEITHER DO I CONDEMN YOU

JOHN 7:53 – 8:11

Leader's briefing

The penultimate session uses one of the most controversial passages in the Gospels. It is not found in most of the ancient manuscripts, and many of the Church Fathers express concern over its portrayal of Jesus. If sin can be dealt with so lightly – 'Then neither do I condemn you' – is this permission to sin with impunity? Yet Jesus also says, 'Go now and leave your life of sin.' How do we square these two things? And, as difficult as it is for us to achieve, we need to consider how we also might act in the same spirit that Jesus displays here.

The passage of the woman caught in adultery raises issues of our own sexual morality and sinfulness. There are plenty of questions and you need to take care that people do not feel coerced into openly confessing past (or current) indiscretions. It is good to bear in mind that the unmarried members of the group may not be virgins, and the married members may carry guilt from pre-marital or adulterous relationships. We need to avoid the extremes of assuming that none of the group members could possibly have fallen into sexual sin, or pressuring anyone to talk about sex in ways that they are uncomfortable with.

The emphasis needs to be on forgiveness, not on titillation. Be prepared for the possibility of a group member choosing this situation to make a very personal confession, but do not try to manipulate it. This is especially the situation with the final meditation: stress that this is intended to be a silent time of personal meditation.

There is also the possibility that some group members may have had relationships break up, and marriage end in divorce because of adultery. Hopefully you will already know if that has been the case, but need to be aware that this may have happened to other relatives of group members.

Ultimately, this passage is shocking for the forgiveness that Jesus extends so readily, but also powerful for the encouragement and comfort it should give all of us, whether we are guilty of sexual sin or not. 'Neither do I condemn you' should warm our hearts as a clear indication of the character of our God. He treats us with grace. This session should help us think about how we also might treat one another with grace.

Preparation

Play CD track 16.

Read John 7:53 – 8:11.

Investigation

1. When Jesus says, 'Let any one of you who is without sin be the first to throw a stone at her', do you think he meant 'without sexual sin' or 'without any sin'? Does it matter?
2. Does this passage support the idea that you can sin with impunity because you can just confess it and be forgiven? If so, how can we avoid that attitude?
3. If sin can be forgiven so easily, why is there any need for punishment?
4. Is it only on matters involving sexual sin that we're likely to turn into Pharisees? What are the situations that most easily provoke our 'righteous' indignation instead of our compassionate understanding?

Observation

Play CD track 17.

Give the group a chance to ask any questions to clarify what they have just heard.

Texts mentioned:

- 'Grace, by definition, is always undeserved' – George Beasley-Murray, *John, Word Biblical Commentary 36*, Word, 1987, p147.

Application

5. Is sexual sin harder to forgive than other sins? If so, why?
6. Is there anything from the earlier sessions to help us when we are faced with the need to forgive sexual sin?
7. Should we feel guiltier about sexual sin than any other sort of sin?
8. Rehabilitating church leaders or lay workers who have committed public sexual indiscretion is difficult. Or perhaps you think it is too

easy? Can it be done, and if so, how should it be? Should such a person ever re-enter church ministry? If not, why not?

9   A common scenario in some films and television programmes is of a character who has been sexually unfaithful being counselled that they are being selfish if they confess this to their spouse. Could that ever be a Christian action, or must Christians always confess sexual sin to their spouse?

Optional question:

10 In the light of this story of the adulterous woman, how has the Church's attitudes to adultery changed in recent times? Does the incident have any insights to offer us about the Church's attitude to homosexuality?

Summary

Play CD track 18.

Texts mentioned:

- 'If this is what God will do for his enemies, how much more will he do for his friends?' – a paraphrase of Romans 5:10: 'For if, when we were God's enemies, we were reconciled to him through the death of his Son, how much more, having been reconciled, shall we be saved through his life!'

- 'The Lord's, "Neither do I condemn you," must be taken as a declaration of forgiveness in the name of God. ...Whoever first recounted the story intended us to understand the word of forgiveness as a means of release to start a new life' – George Beasley-Murray, *John, Word Biblical Commentary 36*, Word, 1987, p147.

Reflection and adoration

For this time we suggest that group members focus on their loved ones past and present. Of course, not everyone in the group will be married: they should focus on their ex-spouse, their fiancé/e or ex-fiancé/e, or people with whom they once had a relationship that they had hoped would lead to marriage but it never did. And, like the woman described in John's Gospel, there may be relationships we are not proud of that God has brought to our attention as the group has been talking and which we now need to acknowledge to him. Again, I stress that this reflection is not a time of pressure for group members to rush to a position of forgiveness for anything that might come from a difficult relationship; but if time is not set aside for this, then the study of forgiveness can remain a cerebral experience, not a life-changing one. You could use Psalm 51 as a meditative reading, especially if there has been an element of confession in your session.

But it is also a moment for people to give thanks for the many positive benefits and blessings that they have experienced from their closest relationships.

Close by singing or reading the words of 'Wonderful grace' by John Pantry © 1990 HarperCollins Religious.

Continuation

There are a number of films that touch on issues of forgiveness and understanding within the realm of sexual sin. Almost inevitably, these films will contain scenes of a sexual nature; the disparity between Christian and worldly values will probably mean that most of us will feel that many of these scenes are gratuitous rather than essential. Those able and willing to try to cope with this, though, will find some of this material thought-provoking.

Our first suggestion is Stanley Kubrick's *Eyes Wide Shut* (1999, 18 certificate). A difficult and disturbing film and, even with the outstanding performances of Tom Cruise and Nicole Kidman, there are still a few weaknesses in the production. However, this is one of few films that not only touches on the theme of forgiveness for adultery but actually portrays people expressing regret and determination to change.

The suggested alternative is *Priest* (2004, 15 certificate). A Roman Catholic priest is caught between his own homosexual yearnings and the confession from one of his child parishioners that she is being sexually abused by her father. If he is to denounce the father in public, should he also 'come out' about his own sexuality, and which of them will receive understanding from the parishioners if he does?

7: THE JOY OF YOUR SALVATION

PSALM 51

Leader's briefing

The final session turns to the well-known Psalm 51. Its clear structure enables us to think about the standard pattern of sin and forgiveness. We need actually to acknowledge that our actions have been sinful, affirm our intention to live according to God's standards, and then ask his forgiveness for the sin.

We will also be thinking about the way in which we might start to think of forgiveness as some sort of an automatic process. There are a number of different ways in which we might take it for granted, not least that of thinking we can 'fudge' our way around it. We might also reduce forgiveness to some sort of formula rather than remembering that it is undeserved and unmerited. In addition, we can take that formula and start to use it as some sort of evaluative tool of the behaviour of other Christians.

More than this, forgiveness is part of a relationship. It is because we are in an ongoing relationship with Christ that we approach him for forgiveness. This should be something that gives us comfort, assurance and joy.

These things have been touched on in various ways throughout the previous sessions; we bring them together as we close to ensure that we finish with a positive appreciation of how gracious God is, and how he calls us to an equal grace.

Preparation

Play CD track 19.

Read Psalm 51.

Investigation

1   In what way does the psalm present a standard logical order for us to follow when dealing with sin?
2   In some senses David's sin had been against Bathsheba and Uriah

(see 2 Samuel 11). In the light of verse 4, how can we ensure we are more aware of the way our sin offends God and not just other people?

3   Is 'the joy of your salvation' (verse 12) an emotional feeling? Or something else?

4   In verse 16 we find the extraordinary statement that God does not delight in sacrifice. What aspects of our religious practice might we rely on and falsely trust in rather than a 'broken and contrite heart'?

Note: A quick glance through the early chapters of Leviticus can give the impression that sacrifice is at the core of the way God expected the Israelites to relate to him. From the regularity of the daily morning and evening sacrifice, to the special sacrifices of specific festivals, it was a continual part of their faith. So the group might well suggest that attending worship on Sunday is a contemporary parallel.

5   In what ways does the psalm express confidence in God's forgiveness?

Note: There are fewer explicit statements than we might presume. In verse 7, the 'I shall be…' statements indicate certainty; and in verse 14, there is the phrase 'the God who saves me'. Otherwise, we would point to the whole mood of the psalm, that it does not come across as uncertain, or 'hoping against hope'. The close (verses 16 and 17), with its rejection of sacrifice, is also significant, for it indicates that (even in the context of the Old Testament) God is more interested in our heart attitude than any action that might somehow 'force' him to forgive us.

Observation

Play CD track 20. Give the group a chance to ask any questions to clarify what they have just heard.

Texts mentioned:

-   Jesus answered, 'I tell you, not seven times, but seventy-seven times' – Matthew 18:22.

Application

6   Do we recognise times in our own lives when we have reduced confession and forgiveness to a formula, rather than valued it as a facet of a relationship with Christ?

7   Joy, relaxation, comfort: what images and pictures of the benefits of a life with Christ do we have?

8   What experiences of the joy of forgiveness would we like to share with one another?

Questions to bring the series to a close:

9   What have we learnt about forgiveness that we feel is especially relevant to us?

10 In the first session, we expressed concerns about the idea that sin might be the least important thing in the Christian life. (We may, as suggested, have kept a written note of them.) Have those issues been addressed in the rest of the sessions? If not, what still needs to be discussed?

Summary

Play CD track 21.

Texts mentioned:

- 'The beginning of wisdom is to know oneself to be a sinner' – Augustine, reported in Peter Craigie, *Psalms 1–50, Word Biblical Commentary*, Word, 1983, p268.
- '… all our righteous acts are like filthy rags' – Isaiah 64:6.
- 'Ransomed, healed, restored, forgiven' – from the hymn 'Praise, my soul, the King of Heaven', by J Goss.
- 'If we confess our sins, he is faithful and just and will forgive us our sins and purify us from all unrighteousness' – 1 John 1:9.

Reflection and adoration

I suggest that for this final time the group might focus on prayer for their siblings. Begin by reading through the Parable of the Prodigal Son in Luke 15:11–32. Invite the group members to think of ways in which they have behaved, thinking not only about the younger son but also about the times when they have acted like the elder son.

Close by singing or reading the words of 'In Christ Alone' by Stuart Townend and Keith Getty © 2001 Thankyou Music or focus entirely on the triumphant words of the fourth verse which begins: 'No guilt in life, no fear in death, This is the power of Christ in me.'

Continuation

The title of our first recommended film readily indicates its significance. *The Grudge* is a horror film available in two versions, both directed by Takashi Shimizu: the Japanese original (2003, 15 certificate) and a Hollywood remake (2004, starring Sarah Michelle Gellar, 15 certificate). A vengeful spirit attacks people who come to the house. The film gradually reveals the reason for the spirit's grudge.

Alternatively, you might prefer *The Fisher King* (1991, director Terry Gilliam, starring Robin Williams and Jack Lucas, 15 certificate). A radio DJ attempts to make amends for a horrible mistake in his past by helping a man deranged by the effects of that mistake. Frequently funny, extremely rude for a few moments, this is enjoyable and thought-provoking in the way it eschews simplistic answers to its own questions.

Photocopiable worksheet

1: CONFESS AND BE FORGIVEN

Reading: 1 John 1:5 – 2:2

Investigation

1. What does John mean by the phrase 'walk in the darkness'? If we commit a single sin does that mean that we are then walking 'in the darkness'? Or does he have something different in mind?

2. What might the people who claimed to be 'without sin' (verses 8 and 10) have understood about the Christian life to have so deluded themselves into genuinely believing this was correct? Alternatively, do we think they were maliciously trying to deceive people?

3. Most of the New Testament letters were written to challenge incorrect ideas that had developed. Looking at the things John writes here, what wrong ideas do we think his audience had started believing?

Optional extra question:

4   In Micah 6:7 we read, 'Shall I offer my firstborn for my transgression, the fruit of my body for the sin of my soul?' What misconceptions about forgiveness and God's requirements of us are common in today's Church?

Application

5   Is it possible to make too much of sin and confession in the Christian life? What might be the dangers of this?

6   Does our local church make too much, or too little, of sin and confession in our services?

7   Does the idea that sin is the *least* important thing in the Christian life mean that we can commit any sins we want?

8   What things, if any, worry us about the idea that sin might be the least important thing in the Christian life? What issues and/or balancing statements would we want to see in later sessions?

9   How would we know if we ought to be paying more (or less) attention to the sin in our lives?

10   What sort of things might make us unwilling to admit even to ourselves that we have sinned?

11   What is the proper role of guilt in the Christian life?

12   Do you think that in his letter John is trying to make us feel guilty about sin?

13 How have we dealt with any guilt we feel even after we have confessed our sins? Without needing to go into details of the sin, would anyone be willing to share what they did to alleviate any lingering sense of guilt?

Photocopiable worksheet

2: TOTAL CONFESSION

Reading: Psalm 32:1–5

Investigation

1. Why might we be unwilling to acknowledge our sin to God? Psychologically speaking, what might be happening to make us reluctant to own up to sin?

2. Does the phrase 'in whose spirit there is no deceit' (verse 2) describe some sort of excellent sinlessness, or does it refer to something else?

3. Have any of us experienced this 'groaning' and 'wasting away' (verse 3)?

4. Is the psalmist describing psychosomatic illness or just using poetic language? Does it matter which it is?

5   What do we think the 'guilt of my sin' (verse 5) is?

6   The **Preparation** audio track also mentioned times when we do not feel any sort of negative emotion about our sins. Can we still be forgiven for them, and – if so – on what basis?

7   Verses 1 and 2 describe a blessed state for those who have sinned and confessed; is this a good motivation for us to confess our sins to God, that we might feel good as a result?

Read Matthew 5:23,24.

8   What contemporary situations would parallel the inconvenience of leaving a sacrifice in order to be reconciled with someone? How far does Jesus expect us to go?

Application

9. Do we recognise ourselves in these attempts to justify not confessing our sins?
   - 'Look, Lord, I've committed this one so often I don't really need to confess it again.'
   - 'I might as well wait until I've committed this one a few more times and then confess them all as a sort of job lot.'

   What other reasons do any of us have for not being willing to confess our sins?

10. How would we define repentance?
    - Is repentance something we do once, when we become Christians, or something that should be a frequent part of the Christian life? Or are they two different things that we could do with different terms for?
    - Is repentance something that comes out of an emotional response to sin, or is it more an intellectual decision?
    - Is repentance the same as remorse and penitence for our sins?
    - What is the difference between asking for forgiveness and repenting?

11. What experience of trusting in the promise in 1 Corinthians 10:13 have we had which we can share with one another?

Photocopiable worksheet

3: CONTINUAL FORGIVENESS

Reading: Matthew 6:12–15; 18:21–35

Investigation

1. Do these two passages teach that we are forgiven our sins *because* we forgive others?

2. Do they teach that God cannot possibly forgive us *unless* we have forgiven others?

3. It seems it was easy for the king/master in Matthew 18 to write off a debt of a million pounds. Do we fall into the same trap of forgiving people when it costs us little (relatively speaking), but holding a grudge when it would be costly for us?

4. In the parable, the debt that needed to be forgiven was financial. What sorts of debts/sins do we find it easy or hard to forgive?

5   In the parable, the king does not forgive the servant a second time. Is that in conflict with the idea that we should forgive 'seventy-seven times' (verse 22)?

Read Luke 17:3b,4. If you have time, you could also read the following verses, which all deal with similar issues: Mark 11:25,26, Ephesians 4:32 and Colossians 3:13.

6   We know Jesus is not asking us to keep a count. Is there anything we've said so far that these verses would challenge us with?

Application

7   So where are our limits on forgiveness, and what might we find it hard to forgive?

8   Is it harder to forgive people who commit sins against our loved ones than to forgive them for sins committed against us personally? Why is that?

9   How do we continue to forgive someone who sins against us so often that we get exasperated with them as they break the 'seventy-seven times' barrier, or sin against us eight times in one day?

10 Does the length of time that's elapsed since a sin was committed make a difference to our ability to forgive?

11 Under what circumstances (if ever) would it be correct to try to force someone to forgive?

12 Thinking back to the previous session, Psalm 32 described the emotional and physical turmoil that might result from not confessing our own sin to God. Is there an equivalent turmoil when we are not prepared to forgive someone?

Photocopiable worksheet

4: MAKING RECOMPENSE

Reading: Luke 19:1–10

Investigation

To start with, a few quick questions on verse 8. Zacchaeus gave away half his possessions and paid back fourfold the money he had cheated people of.

1   Did Jesus ask him to do this?

2   Was he forgiven *because* he did it? If not, why – then – did he do it?

3   What role does making recompense have to play in Christian forgiveness?

Application

4   Zacchaeus voluntarily paid compensation for the sin of cheating people out of money. What kind of sins committed by people today might need to be accompanied by some sort of compensation if forgiveness is to be extended?

5   Is there a difference between forgiveness and restoration, and (if so) how does it help us better understand forgiveness?

6   If someone who has committed a crime that ought to be reported to the police asks for forgiveness, should we still report that crime?

7   Do we have the right to ask for some sort of compensation before we are willing to forgive someone?

8   'I just want to pay the price and move on.' Are there times when we simply cannot deal with our sins and failures just by making recompense?

9   In the previous session we heard the idea that people sometimes say, 'I'll never forgive you for that.' Have any of us ever had that said to us, and, if so, what did we do (if anything) to try to make good the damage and hurt?

_____

_____

_____

10 Will anyone in the group admit to having said, 'I'll never forgive you/him/her for that'? Do they still feel the same way?

_____

_____

_____

Photocopiable worksheet

5: FORGIVEN MUCH, LOVE MUCH

Reading: Luke 7:36–50

Investigation

1. There is a lot of money mentioned in this narrative: a debt of 500 denarii (nearly two years' wages), a debt of 50 denarii (about two months' wages) and an alabaster jar of perfume that in Mark 14:5 is stated as being worth more than a year's wages. What would be an equivalent of a jar of perfume?

2. Do you think the woman has already experienced forgiveness, and wishes to express her gratitude to Jesus, or has she come seeking forgiveness?

3. Is Jesus' parable an absolute statement about forgiveness and love that is applicable in each and every single situation to everyone, or is it one composed for the situation to help Simon see that the woman behaved this way out of gratitude? What difference does it make?

4   Is Jesus telling us to believe that some sins are minor in God's eyes?

5   What ways of misreading the parable can we see?

6   Has our discussion and understanding of forgiveness in any way compromised the straight-forward statement of 1 John 1:8,9? If so, what alterations do we need to acknowledge?

Application

Questions focusing on forgiveness after crimes:

7   What response would we give to the prisoner who finds his attempts at expressing repentance ignored?

8   In what sense are we required to forgive someone who has not committed their sin against us personally? Would there be mileage in suggesting that some sins are so public that they impact an entire society?

9   When Myra Hindley died, the *Sun* newspaper celebrated the event by declaring its confidence that she was now in hell. Is our ability to forgive someone such as Hindley an appropriate litmus test of our ability to forgive?

10 Which of these other categories of people challenge our ability to forgive them?
    – suicide bombers
    – IRA bombers
    – paedophiles
    – wife batterers

11 What other crimes do we find especially difficult to forgive?

12   There have been a number of public apologies (or not) for acts of violence that took place decades or centuries ago, normally concerning the Holocaust, American slave trade or the Crusades. Does this give us a model for confession of sins we did not commit (but benefit from) and forgiveness of sins committed against others in our society?

13   Presuming that Myra Hindley genuinely repented and asked God to forgive her, is there any reason for believing that she was not forgiven? What are the implications that arise from that?

General questions:

14   Is it essential to have committed (and been forgiven for) 'great' sins in order to 'love much'? Is it enough to be aware of an increasing number of 'minor' sins?

15   How do we stop ourselves becoming blasé about our forgiveness?

16 Is it possible to say we have been forgiven if the person we have wronged refuses to forgive us?

17 Have we hurt people in the past by deliberately refusing to forgive them for something?

18 'My chains fell off, my heart was free; I rose, went forth, and followed Thee' (from 'And can it be', Charles Wesley's hymn). Should we think of ourselves as bound in chains whenever we need to be forgiven, or is it only something that was true of our pre-Christian state?

Photocopiable worksheet

6: NEITHER DO I CONDEMN YOU

Reading: John 7:53 – 8:11

Investigation

1. When Jesus says, 'Let any one of you who is without sin be the first to throw a stone at her', do you think he meant 'without sexual sin' or 'without any sin'? Does it matter?

2. Does this passage support the idea that you can sin with impunity because you can just confess it and be forgiven? If so, how can we avoid that attitude?

3. If sin can be forgiven so easily, why is there any need for punishment?

4. Is it only on matters involving sexual sin that we're likely to turn into Pharisees? What are the situations that most easily provoke our 'righteous' indignation instead of our compassionate understanding?

Application

5   Is sexual sin harder to forgive than other sins? If so, why?

6   Is there anything from the earlier sessions to help us when we are faced with the need to forgive sexual sin?

7   Should we feel guiltier about sexual sin than any other sort of sin?

8   Rehabilitating church leaders or lay workers who have committed public sexual indiscretion is difficult. Or perhaps you think it is too easy? Can it be done, and if so, how should it be? Should such a person ever re-enter church ministry? If not, why not?

9   A common scenario in some films and television programmes is of a character who has been sexually unfaithful being counselled that they are being selfish if they confess this to their spouse. Could that ever be a Christian action, or must Christians always confess sexual sin to their spouse?

Optional question:

10 In the light of this story of the adulterous woman, how has the Church's attitudes to adultery changed in recent times? Does the incident have any insights to offer us about the Church's attitude to homosexuality?

Photocopiable worksheet

7: THE JOY OF YOUR SALVATION

Reading: Psalm 51

Investigation

1. In what way does the psalm present a standard logical order for us to follow when dealing with sin?

   _____

   _____

   _____

2. In some senses David's sin had been against Bathsheba and Uriah (see 2 Samuel 11). In the light of verse 4, how can we ensure we are more aware of the way our sin offends God and not just other people?

   _____

   _____

   _____

3. Is 'the joy of your salvation' (verse 12) an emotional feeling? Or something else?

   _____

   _____

   _____

4. In verse 16 we find the extraordinary statement that God does not delight in sacrifice. What aspects of our religious practice might we rely on and falsely trust in rather than a 'broken and contrite heart'?

   _____

5   In what ways does the psalm express confidence in God's forgiveness?

Application

6   Do we recognise times in our own lives when we have reduced confession and forgiveness to a formula, rather than valued it as a facet of a relationship with Christ?

7   Joy, relaxation, comfort: what images and pictures of the benefits of a life with Christ do we have?

8   What experiences of the joy of forgiveness would we like to share with one another?

Questions to bring the series to a close:

9   What have we learnt about forgiveness that we feel is especially relevant to us?

10 In the first session, we expressed concerns about the idea that sin might be the least important thing in the Christian life. (We may, as suggested, have kept a written note of them.) Have those issues been addressed in the rest of the sessions? If not, what still needs to be discussed?

DEEPER ENCOUNTER

- Bible study material for confident small groups
- Written by John Wilks, Director of Open Learning, London School of Theology
- 7 sessions in each book, with CD audio tracks and photocopiable worksheets

Other titles in this series:

SLOW TO ANGER – This recurrent theme from the Scriptures is often overlooked yet it has much to say to us about the unchanging character of God and how we relate to him.

PLAYING SECOND FIDDLE – Our understanding of our faith will not flourish if we ignore the problems of real life. An exploration of Romans 12 gives us a valuable basis for establishing values and making decisions.

LOVE ONE ANOTHER – So simple yet so profound; this command pervading John's Letters and Gospel stretches us in our community life and helps us take a fresh look at our discipleship.

KNOWING CHRIST CRUCIFIED – A sacrificed lamb, a ransom for sin, a substitute for death, an appeaser of God's wrath; this study explores many of the Scriptural images which give deeper insights into why Jesus died.

SERVE THE LORD – The experiences of Abraham, Joseph, Jeremiah, Stephen, Paul and others provide the context for looking at calling or vocation. Can the Christian working on the supermarket checkout or caring for children at home be said in any sense to be exercising a ministry?

Scripture Union also publishes **church@home**, a free online magazine about the world of small groups. Go to www.scriptureunion.org.uk/churchathome

Also recommended:

ENCOUNTER WITH GOD

The ideal quarterly Bible reading guide for the thinking Christian who wants to interpret and apply the Bible in a way that is relevant to the issues of today's world. Daily comments from an international team of writers plus supporting features. Available from all Christian bookshops. Please contact Scripture Union for a free sample back issue.

To ask for a free sample, order or enquire about any of our publications:

- phone SU's mail order line: 0845 070 6006
- email info@scriptureunion.org.uk
- log on to www.scriptureunion.org.uk
- write to SU Mail Order, PO Box 5148, Milton Keynes MLO, MK2 2YX